BANGALEE

Written by:
STEPHEN COSGROVE

Illustrated by:
ROBIN JAMES

A Serendipity Book

Dedicated to Ron Pederson and Joe Stout, the original Kritters.

Steve

In a very dusty corner of a very confused land stood a jumbled up pile of rocks and rubble called Kritter Castle. All around the castle was litter of all sorts. There were tires and cans, bottles and bells, and all sorts of ugly, dirty garbage.

Inside this castle of rust and ruin lived some furry little creatures called Kritters. A Kritter was like no other animal you have ever seen. It had short furry legs, short furry arms, and a fat furry face that was always dirty. For, you see, the only thing Kritters could do well was to be messy.

They never combed their hair, never washed their faces and you would always find their clothes in the strangest of places.

Day in and day out they would dash about the castle littering here and littering there. They would drop their candy wrappers, gum wrappers, newspapers anywhere they happened to be. Because of all the junk lying around, never a day would go by without one of the Kritters slipping or tripping on a pile of garbage. Fortunately, they would usually end up falling on a pile of discarded rags and luckily never hurt themselves.

In the middle of this castle of confusion there was one room that was absolutely, sparkling clean. It was here that the cleanest of all the Kritters lived and he was called Bangalee.

He was short and furry just like all the other Kritters except that his face was always clean, his hair was always combed, and you would never find him wearing dirty clothes.

Bangalee would constantly zip about his room picking up his toys, putting away his clothes and dusting every nook and cranny. He would wash the windows, wash the walls and sometimes even vacuum the halls. Bangalee was so clean and organized that he was the one creature in the whole world who could always find that spot you always miss.

All the other Kritters would just laugh and call Bangalee names because no matter where he went he would polish the lamps, clean the chairs, wipe the windows and wash the stairs.

But, no sooner would he finish his chores than a whole mess of Kritters would walk by kicking up dust and dirt and poor Bangalee would have to start all over again.

He became so frustrated that one day he stood in the middle of the castle square and called for all the Kritters to gather around.

"My fellow Kritters," he began when they had arrived, "wouldn't it be nice to live in a neat and clean castle?"

"Aw, pooh!" one of them muttered. "A little litter never hurt anyone." With that the motley group went on its way mumbling and grumbling, leaving Bangalee a bigger mess than when he had started.

Things would have gone on this way forever had it not been for the Grunk. The Grunk was a monstrous garbage-eating beast who had been wandering around the countryside for many years looking for something to eat. Since Kritter Castle was the junkiest place around, it was only natural that he would come here for a super-big feast.

When the Kritters caught sight of the Grunk they ran inside the castle and quickly tried to raise the drawbridge. But there was so much garbage in the way, they could only get it closed halfway.

Fortunately, there was so much litter outside that the Grunk began to eat it first. He ate some tires that had sat there so long, and he even ate a bell that had lost its gong.

"Oh, what are we to do?" they cried. "The Grunk eats junk and we're so dirty that he'll probably eat us too!" They began running here and there, looking for someplace to hide, but no matter where they looked there was garbage and litter and no safe place to hide.

Finally Bangalee came forward and said, "I think I have a plan that will save us from the Grunk." With muddy tears streaming from their eyes the Kritters all gathered around. "The only thing the Grunk wants is junk. If we clean up our rooms and clean up the streets and throw all the garbage outside for the Grunk to eat, then he will have no reason to come inside the castle and we will be safe."

The Kritters agreed and set out to clean the castle. They picked up the paper, the bottles, the cans that were lying on the ground, and then they washed the walls that were dirty and brown. They picked up the toys in their rooms and hung up their clothes, then washed off the street by using a hose.

Load after load of garbage was thrown out of the castle to the waiting Grunk. Finally there wasn't a speck of garbage or litter left in the rooms or in the square. For the first time in many, many years the castle was clean.

That Grunk had never seen so much junk. He ate the dirt, the rags, the newspapers all, and he even ate an old rubber ball. When he had eaten all there was to eat, he sniffed and sniffed but there just wasn't anymore.

With a belch and a burp he lumbered away from the castle in search of more garbage and junk.

The Kritters all shouted and cheered as the Grunk disappeared. Then they stopped and looked around. The castle, which had been so junky and messy, was now so clean that it sparkled in the afternoon sunlight.

"If the castle can look so good after being cleaned up, maybe if you all took a bath, you could feel just as good," suggested Bangalee.

The Kritters looked at each other covered with dust and grime and proclaimed that from this day forth dirt would be a crime. So all the Kritters from the very old to the very young took a hot, soapy bath and got clean to the bone.

To this very day Kritter Castle is clean and the junky old Grunk has never been seen again.

SO, IF YOUR ROOM IS MESSY
AND CLUTTERED WITH
   LOTS OF JUNK,
BETTER CLEAN UP YOUR ROOM
   LIKE BANGALEE
'CAUSE HERE COMES THE GRUNK!